1969

This book may be kept

SUMMER UNBOUND

a publication of the Amy Lowell
Travelling Scholarship Fund

Summer unbound

AND OTHER POEMS

by E. L. MAYO

the university of minnesota press

FOR DOUGLAS BUSH

table of contents

PART I · PLACES

the house on pleasant street

Nobody
Lived there in my time. The ground was full
Of granite outcroppings — and walking by
Alone in late November in the rain

You knew the tangled grass was all rock under.
Its wooden domes and cupolas had grown
Gray through and through, and there were several signs,
KEEP OFF, NO TRESPASSING, as gray as they,

But in the high top windows there was still
Glass to catch the sunsets. You might say,
"Someone is in. How soon their lights are on!"
Until you looked again. They pulled it down

Because it was too big for anyone,
And the employed built for the unemployed
A terraced park there. Lonely walkers now
No longer smell sweet-grass and mullein-weed

Rankling in the rain like an old wound
But sweet deodorant from the comfort station,
And caretakers complain
Of lovers and newspapers on the lawn.

granite city

The granite sidewalks and the granite warrens
Of granite houses on the granite hills
Keep them warm enough, and roses, roses
Still in October, still now in November
Charge their back gardens, dooryards, window sills.

Every stoop is scrubbed to the mineral bone;
Every lamppost holds a basket up
For wastepaper and newspaper. Bars and such
Dissolute lackeys to dissolving nature
Lurk in back alleys, close at half past nine.

Calvin incarnated in granite here
What Euclid crystallized, and precious time
(Since every steeple has a clock in it)
And God are one, and man predestinate
To a good tombstone. Tombstones anyway

Are a flourishing local industry,
And many an aging Aberdonian
In Lima, Vladivostok, or Cape Town
Orders his tombstone here who does not know
How much rock is shipped from Norway now.

For the gleaming town between the Dee and the Don
Is running out of granite, but the year
She carves her final weapon in the war
Of wind and rain with memory, the rose
Will storm her steeples and be conqueror.

londoners

hate the past. Only Americans
get excited about it. If you're strangled
with cold castles and monuments to the dead
good and bad clutter the public ways
and forms for filling fill your nights and days
you don't necessarily love them because they are there.

Still, there they are: you stand in a queue and stare
at miles of chimney pots and masonry
and say: I live here, I have lived here
in soot, chill, patience, and courtesy
and the cool of the Thames of a summer evening
eating a bun on a bench watching the shipping,

and glory too, of course, but glory has
gravity and does not move so fast
as citizens of the United States past
craters between building and building
and old solidities no longer there:
there are no bomb-holes in America.

postwar landscape

Insulate, unhyssoped, shy of song,
These strong and clever hands stretched out toward good
Weave Egypt over gardens
They will not see, they cannot seed. The world
Soots over; only barracks and airport
Shine clear, and in an hour
These, too, will all be sooted over. Only
The sky's delicate, soft-coal-smoke gray
Is real, and all production fawns on war.
Lear's little dogs, Tray, Blanche, and Sweetheart, see
How they bark! Who is the running man?
Allons enfants! the telescreen within
Instructs the children in the Master Plan.
And all who thought to find
Love in the waste of time between wars
Or clambering the mind's interstices
In catch-as-catch-can liberty, some wind
Frank, cold, blowing for unknown seas,
Gnaw the cotton bread of unison;
For when they are alone
The thundering engine of the mechanical heart
Laboring to lift the world above the world
By pure force, screams in their ears, and song
Ceases, or if it start
Hardens in the hardening of art.

twinkling

Under the sullen of a Surrey fall
Let sun but for a moment well and spill
Out of the overcast, and every door
(How bright they paint their doors!) and every flower —
Wildflower, bush, and beech-leaf suddenly are
Wild with the colors of Jerusalem.

John's Vision, quick as a cat's claw
Snatches you in, and there
Shining with every gem and precious stone
Stands the Indelible City Blake saw
In the pulsation of an artery
And in another, gone.

hometown

Malden, city of my dead youth,
City of tired sleepers and no glories,
Detoured by Paul Revere, where Sacco's ghost
Wails round the Baptist Church; city of Judson,
Bringer of light to Burma, who dying there
Never knew how dark it grew elsewhere;

City of Sunday mornings deep with bells
Where under elms and maples with my father
I walked to a church that smelt of damp plaster
(I thought it then the smell of rectitude)
And one day heard my pretty Sunday School teacher
Tell how they crucified Christ and when I cried
Somebody kicked me hard under the table.

City of Cross Street, city of Suffolk Square,
The ghetto where an older man I knew
Bought pumpernickel — he was a Christian, too —
And jam and cream cheese, traded with a Jew
Because he liked the man. The neighbors said
He read too much and wasn't all there,

But when the fog rolled up from the Lynn Marsh
And Linden and Revere and we went in,
Beside the Mystic River he had seen
A vision of our City where the sun
Of Campanella, Booker Washington,
Veblen, and Lincoln Steffens, and Einstein
Shines equally on every honest man.

occupied territory

We are not the first
Inhabitants, the sole proprietors,
Nor thrid the mazes of the Minotaur

With lucky string. Nature is innocent
Of nothing, nothing. Only a tissue thin
Curtain in the brain shuts out the coiled

Recumbent Landlord. Lift it and look there,
There where among huge alien stones the hawk
Leans to the singular scream of the struck hare.

PART II · LETTERS AND ENCOUNTERS

apparition

Sun, moon, and stars forever stalking me,
Give me a sense of nakedness. It is
Hard for one so much in the public eye
To be perfectly natural. Nevertheless,
As I strolled out this evening minding my business

And trying to put the best possible face on things,
My stick (I am, unfortunately, blind)
Encountered this resilient projection.
I poked again, and then, the wind veering,
Gave up a most unpleasant exhalation.

The odor would have turned me, but the corpse,
Shuddering, trembling, stirring,
Screamed in the shattering
Way they have: "Away! Get away! Leave me
To contemplate the facts of my condition

Without your apparition. Of all things,
What starts my eyes and freezes up my marrow
Most is blind, bodiless, gray
Specters like you!" With an apology,
I backed away. How shall we love each other,

When, as they say in volumes on theology,
We embrace on Resurrection Day?

tapestry

FOR MYRA MAYO

Lady, my love and all my sole desire,
Ruling our harsh antagonist, Rumor's
Ugly tongues, with the strong skill you have,
Love and sustainer of the triple loves
That love us and are loved more than the tongue's
Power to utter — caught in a mystery
That weaves their little loves through iron wires

That spring may leap magnanimous with flowers
Beyond the tongues of prophecy, and grass
Softer than eyelashes of head-on-arm
Children asleep from play. The Unicorn's
Flickering silver lightning and the roar
Of my Gold Lion guard your garden, Lady.
Oh all my senses are

Yours, smell, touch, taste, see, hear what I may
And in your rich pavilion, jewelry
Rarer than all the gems of India spreads
Astonishment. That you weave this for me
Puzzles the world, but the Artificer
Who weaves the world, from his high Judgment Seat
Where tongue, eye fail, commends your tapestry.

to a friend teaching in the provinces

FOR JOHN DOYLE

As you say, John, it is narrowing
And cold, and if the soul was ever sublime
It has forgotten where and what it was,
"Peace" rhymes with "cease." Was there another rhyme?

Bombs help, but we never needed them to tell
What we have learned of apples above all:
Gravitation made the apple fall
With the connivance of a certain worm

That nibbled Newton too, and nibbles
Us and our green ball till every star
Slips like popcorn to explosion.
Therefore we fight. This is the true war

Fought in the narrow skull's, the heavy heart's
Remotest provinces, and we are sent
Against the universal coils with fire
To light the dull, warm the intelligent.

the return of prospero

Prospero, bury that big book
Fifty fathom deep, and turn, turn
Back to Milan: responsibility
Up to the waist, up to the lips again.

They nudge each other, say Look, Look,
His beard is hawthorne and his crown is gold,
And you possess the world
In double sovereignty having the popular will.

But Ariel, the adorable potentate
Who whipped waves wild or made them rear
Back on themselves and sleep, is ransomed now
And Caliban raised to a million

Your proper study. Magic was a kind
Of politics but less empirical,
For things above have their equation
In things below, as water, fire, and air;

But since the Demon fouled
Sycorax, man is ruled by man —
Even by the True Prince, even in Milan —
Somewhere between despair and miracle.

letter to too many people

Now — as if it mattered: there are so many people
    writing so many poems — I write to you
To say that everyone is still
    very well, although
Somewhat beside themselves, there being more to do
    than they can do, and airplane pilots higher
    up in the air than we are
    look freer.
Feet, feet, feet, feet, feet
For all their being cocked up in evening's seat
    are never quite rested by morning any more,
    and hair
    grows rare.
Friends that I miss,
I think there's something specious in all this.
And so I set my face
    rigidly (but secretly of course)
    against the whole elaborate apparatus
    designed, or so I guess, from the very first
    simply to wear us out.
"The more angels the more room," said Swedenborg
    and the machines
    in rubber factories that wear out tires
    almost instantaneously say the same thing
    and all our bonfires
    of sugar, coffee, potatoes, human beings
    so bright they can be seen in Asia
    with peculiar distinctness.

Too many people see by these contents
        the American way
        of living graciously.
It is very simple what these people see;
But not knowing which were the greater courtesy,
to tell truth or make you a little happier,
I mutter beside myself uncertainly
as a bull in a china shop, a lion among ladies,
        a monkeywrench
        or, as the English say,
        more elegantly, a spanner
in man's most delicate machinery:
        honesty in a letter.

homage to vincent

Pass, painter of proud Europe's summer, down
Mind-twisted ways to Torquemada-brown
Hecatombs of leaves and summer's end.
Let grass and clover intermixed with weeds
Incise, and the deft, delicate roots of trees

Gather up your wound. The flickering hordes
Of blackbirds that attacked your ripened grain
And all those insupportable evergreens
That whispered at your back have their reward:
The yoke is lifted from your neckbone.

And that proud Europe that possessed your ear
Slumbers in sorrow on her bloody arm.
Over the puddles of her abattoir
The lean days draw immitigably down,
But on her fortresses and cold cafés

Your stars, enormous and compassionate,
Like sunflowers still undiminished shine;
And in her glory's late
Babylonian captivity
Your lunacy alone ordered her mind.

the sleeping beauty

In a place where hunchbacks and old women
Quarreled in their thin voices all the day
This temporizing grew intolerable:
I knew that here the Sleeping Beauty lay.

(Had they known it all the time and been
Sly servitors where I could only seize
Bad temper and distorted images?)
Sight ended the old argument. I saw

Her tower clear against the star-picked blue
Over their hovels. It was no affair
Of a cloud and the moon's subtle conjunction; thorns
Hatched me all criss-cross as I hacked my way through

And stumbled bloody still and breathing still
Into a country where no footsteps fall
And where from moat, to keep, to citadel
Spider-webs lie like water.

I silvered as I entered through the door
Where time cannot prevail
But howls outside forever where I found her
Asleep, beautiful, the cobwebs round her.

poem for gerard

Understand too late? Of course we can:
The love of everything, like winnowing,
Scatters the spirit like fine dust, plum-bloom
Over the world. Heart must be held, held down
Of its own will, chained, hooded and become
Deaf to itself and dumb

To hear things speak themselves in their sole tongue.
By stress and instress are their songs wrung
Out of them, scaped and bruited; to possess
Their breathing outwardness the eye must go
In to their root and onward to their end
Perishing with their vanishing to span

From germ to the full grain
Mountain or martyr, chestnut-leaf or man.
It makes the blood run cold, warm flesh glower
To think of you, Windhover,
Cleaving so bleak a wind, maneuvering
Sight more than any in how sealed an hour.

the prince of odd
and anger

FOR DYLAN THOMAS

The Prince of Odd and Anger,
The Contrary King's son —
No foster child I sing —
Could do anything
Except betray the lust
Overreaching dust
And the laconic worm
To raise up to the sun
Incorruptible rhyme.

Our wooden leg of words
Sprouts his green leaf sadly
That burgeoned and skipped gladly
Under his regimen.
Whatever *we* had done,
The sooner if done badly,
If better done, yet soon
He took a counter-path
Into the sullen wood.

Now in multitude
We revel in a garden
Eye had never seen
In all Arden
When winds are in the North
But for his setting forth.

to the archpoet

On bulls, and wearing roses,
The men with varnished faces,
The boys who never were young
Stripped for the tired town.

"But you," the nightwind said,
"Be night; pretend you're dead;
Yet listen, shivering, chill,
For April and her bird.

"Despair, Despair, Despair
Nibbles flake by flake
That dainty carrousel
Art for Art's Sake. Go wear

"Sackcloth beneath your neat
Business suit; go eat
Hunger for your meat
With the most elegant air.

"Let the mad old, the dead young
Behave their have, but you,
Attentive to the throe
Of the nightwind, O

"Archpoet and polymath,
Become what you have heard:
A mouth without a tongue
Singing contrition in

"A world without a word."

letter to my grandfather's picture

When you were a boy, Grandfather, you lived on a farm
Sturdily, and, as soon as you could,
Homesteaded, and had a farm of your own.
But slavery? You chose the Cavalry
(You spelt it "Calvary"), one leg for two,
The City, and a little jewelry store;
The factory at last. You died of a stroke
Down at the Mill, fixing the factory clock,

And fixed it very well. That Mill
Has knitted now till every boy and girl
Enters it as the world. The spindles
Carry the yarn in zigzags and tilted angles
Which enters every color under heaven
And leaves but one. You took your time a little
In your day, Grandfather, but now the whistle
Whistles Sundays, holidays, and all.

You wouldn't pray, they say, after the war
But read *The Law of Psychic Phenomena*
Hoping perhaps — being a watchmaker —
To find whatever mainspring made things go.
Then the clock struck. As you climbed up the ladder
Viewing the loom's perspective altogether,
Did all that speeding yarn outline a figure,
A hanging figure, hanging in pain? or can

This be glimpsed only from flat on the floor?
And is it finished on some other floor?

We never see the thing we have worked on
Whirling from revolution to revolution
Through the Mill's long explosion.
Yet do not lean out of the picture, Grandfather;
Though you cried out like Jesus and Jehovah
I could not hear you through the spindles' roar.

PART III · MYTHS AND ENACTMENTS

the monitor reports

The man who will cut his throat, and the man who will twist
From some high office-building window kissed
The girl who will end in a gas oven one of these days.
The bartender, who will die of psittacosis
At the age of 80, served them with Four Roses
Knowing better than they do what it is.

Then there entered in the sad young man
In a gray overcoat who does not know
That every living room and every bar
In all the world contains a time machine.
He was timidly smiling. Every customer
Eyed him with horror, shuddered to recognize

Such ignorance of the future in a face:
It was an insult to the human race
To contemplate the withering-away
With eyes so hideous with hope — as if
All were not finished to the end of time
To the last foreseen eyelash, charted breath.

Then Razor-throat, reacting sharply, said:
"Slice me in segments!" The Jumper only snored:
"Drop dead!" into his seventh glass.
Only the fair asphyxiate to be,
Into her monitored, unprivate wire,
Promptly reported the anomaly,

Saying: "It is a breach of our known fate,
Your guaranty of withering-away
Which is our peace. How can we sleep at night
Dogged by the Unstatistical Man? To me
(These were her actual words in black and white)
It smacks of outright immortality."

the gentle people

The Gentle People said, "We've too much power
Of traction for an overt act of war,"
And drew together in a bomb-shelter
To hobble violent Nature and become
Still in the heart of Pandemonium.

They voted to become invisible
And wear a gray, impenetrable caul
Over their faces while their shoulders
Propped the heavy hills, the hanging hours
That hid their Occupation from our eyes.

Protestant within, unreconciled
To what the Eye sees upon this star
That the Heart cannot know, they stilled and still
Likerous tides in the full moon. I fear
The world revolves more slowly every year.

We shall not feel the weapon in the hands
The Gentle People lay upon our lands
Till pitchers broken at the cistern fill
With fullness over, the Daughters of Music sing,
There is no more sea, the sun stands still.

the gracious ones

The poor things wear
Thin, and very often I suppose
Grow very hungry. It's hard in the sun's glare
(And neon's glare) to fear the Gracious Ones.
Living and dying
More brilliantly than moths or butterflies
Or those small, moving, asymmetrical
Lights called stars that fade out every morning,
We fly and burn, and only
Science fiction or a murder tale
Makes us wonder, *Are they faithful?*

Even our well-mannered children
Are noisier, more fractious far than these,
And when they sleep and give us a moment's peace,
Before we look, before we realize,
The heavy lids of our eyes
Fall, cover us. Come now, Gracious Ones,
Now while the still finger-propped avalanche
Hangs suspended, seize
This passing hour to harrow and accuse.
Censure us as you please.

As to this rumor of a victory, none
Really believe the King will ever return;
And if at last, swollen with plunder,
He should come home, naturally we
Must do what seems best for the family.

What crime is it, and what
Expiation falls, what proper doom
On folks who have but tried to set in order
And make a house a home?

Such is our story. Every citizen
Will witness us in this. Are you deaf? dumb?
Furies? or out walking? or asleep?
Walk softly, then, and if you slumber, breathe
Quietly and do not let your drone
Penetrate the painted nursery door
Where Electra clasps her teddy-bear,
And small Orestes, the day's battle won,
Sleeps with dead soldiers and a plastic gun.

ptyx

Sur les crédences, au salon vide: nul Ptyx,
Aboli bibelot d'inanité sonore
(Car le maître est alle puiser des pleurs au Styx
Avec ce seul objet dont le Néant s'honore).
— Mallarmé

"Hold this!" I held it. We were outside Time
In the cold and the dark and trying to get in.
Just then something gave, and there I was
In broad daylight holding this instrument.
You were cavorting all over the meadow
In hot, strong sun. I called but you were gone
Across the brook, beyond the apple trees
Where I could just make out the smoke of chimneys.

Now the trinket that I held in my hand
Was obsolete, a thing of empty sound,
A worn and dusty Ptyx; yet this alone
Had sprung the barrier and throbbing screen
That on this side seems but a manhole cover,
But under, all the difference between
Time and not-Time. I stood there missing you
More than the morning light could understand.

For you had sloughed me and the Ptyx too
For spaciousness and the world's multitude,
Not doubting for a moment that all good,
Naked, and all real, waited in Time
Where now you hunted it. The gold sun
Shone on the Ptyx, and as I held it there
With summer a foregone conclusion
The whole green meadow called it sinister.

33

For "Who," said buttercup and timothy,
And "Who," the tree toads in strict antiphon,
And "Who," the rich rocks and established trees,
"Would make a mock of such an afternoon
Or pry beyond it to the crack of doom?"
I knew, but held my tongue thinking of your
Odyssey of admiration
And the rich circle of your willed return.

So I held the Ptyx till rock shadows
Stretched like elastic and the last apple
Hanging unpicked, pecked at by birds, fell
And plashed to cider under the feet of cattle,
Till Fall's far-flung auroral rhetoric
Faded and set, the black cat got my tongue,
And in the gunny-sack of the world's night
The Great Bear, all seven stars blazing, hung

And hangs gazing over my left shoulder.
Always I clutch the Ptyx, contented now
To gather in it a few Stygian tears.
(They polarize on earth.) Nothing's sole honor,
The Ptyx, alone considers what it is
Ice cannot find, alone can spring the cover
That closes all. The hunt is over: Hunter
Who once at dayspring cried "Hold this," *hold this.*

the coming of the toads

"The very rich are not like you and me,"
Sad Fitzgerald said, who could not guess
The coming of the vast and gleaming toads
With precious heads, which, at a button's press,
The flick of a switch, hop only to convey
To you and me and even the very rich
The perfect jewel of equality.

making your poem

Begin it only if you must. At first
You'll surely miss the poem at which you aim,
Then hit it perfectly some other time
When you are aiming elsewhere. You will find
Everything coming out quite different.
To your astonishment the reader's mind
Will change it imperceptibly, and then
The poem itself will seem to you to disdain
You and your sweating thought — it's a wise poem
Knows its own father. I've had one
Cut me dead in the street. A poem solves
Only itself, serves but itself, and he
Who makes one can never go back again
To what he was, nor yet be poetry.

one

The unstable lights in the sky, the unaccountable
Behavior of dials and all clocks proclaim
Time's end — and no one is responsible.
With many a chipped chime and cracked gong
Towers toll the end of balancing
Power against power, and arranging
Cleverly, with the utmost energy,
The matter of our last humiliation.

No one is responsible. All, all
Have excellent reasons. Has no Irishman
In the blind language of the setting sun
Told its coming on? Have no wise men
Patiently following a wizened star
Through the all-seeing Eye on Palomar
Reported in the patined sky no pattern
But the pattern of Process unwinding a snapped spring?

No. It is certain the slow dust will fur
Man, his machine; mouse, his breadcrumb
And in these sleeping streets no flickering
Telescreen or cry of baby can
Waken the world unless the brazen bird
Called Chanticleer, in perfect doom's domain,
Crow in the grasp of his delusion
Crow to bring up the sun till one man
Waken, and weep, and hear the clocks strike ONE.

the myth and the makers

Pomp, circumstances, varying lords, or a lass
Run every world-Atlas
On his own sword in the end, where, unlike Charles,
It never occurs to him to apologize
For his unconscionable time a-dying.
The purple slowly pumping out of him,
An Antony for pure amazement cries,
"I'm dying, Egypt, dying!"

No god, no god; and yet the tawny queen
Who taught her weeping to the crocodile
Found sweet the venom of a mothered worm
For lack of him. Because an Antony
Dies as he has lived, largely;
Empires crumble where his knees give way,
Chasm where he hits, and all his loves
Buckle in landslides to his open grave.

What is this "greatness" that a change in the wind,
The fluctuation of a lady's mind
Should shuck the world, and mere Ability
With a head for double-entry bookkeeping
Re-possess, re-finish, put it on?
Look about you at their sufferings then
And hear poor Tom and Nan wearily pray:
Good Lord deliver us from Great Men.

Yet in a month ploughed under Antony
Stumbles in vulgar verse; the balladeers
Heave him aloft on Fortune's Ferris Wheel;
Shoe-clerks ponder him between pay days.

Wherever Hope turns in a hopeless maze
Antony stirs. First the green blade
That looks like grain, and then the ear of steel,
And then the harvest, red, corruptible

And all is as it was. Who builds these tall
Myths-in-the-flesh, omniresponsible
To myth as to their millions millionaires?
What are their names to whom all in the world
Not noble to the bone, purple in grain
Is fiat paper, pious fraud, and weighs
Less than a feather on the scale of days
Against one careless shrug of Antony's?

They are cold Tom and hungry Nan
Who on this world's flat screen
Project in shining fourth dimension
Fate cannot reach or bend, an Antony
Scattering kings like nickels from his hands
And, fishing off the docks with him, his Queen
To light through coughs, bad air, gum wrappers thrown,
Their trudge through the alone to the alone.

the ringing

In your hand; it is within your hand
And therefore inaccessible and you
Also walk the Valley of Desolation
Among the thousand thousands.

                It is more
Than flesh can bear; it breaks under it; therefore
So many and so many in the night
Dream their tomb, assuming in the dream
The prenatal posture.

                There was a teacher,
Once, who in a blackboard found a door
Into a garden, into a green garden,
And everyone who wished could enter there.
Then the bell rang.

                It is still ringing.
The patient, tolerant substance
Of which we make our tables and our chairs
Has not heard it and is in the garden
Through our conversation,

                  And through
Our longest wars steel itself is still.
Bird, insect, dog, everything animal
Knows this, and if they look at us at all
Look sadly at us

                Over the warm wall —
Excluded not by pang or any pain
(They pay as gladly for the beautiful
As we do), but this endlessly clanging bell.

40

PART IV · MODES

the dial and the mole

(IN MEMORIAM: SIMONE WEIL, 1909–1943)

> What the common basis was, both at home
> and abroad is not easy to define. In those days
> it was unnecessary to formulate it; at the
> present time it becomes impossible to formu-
> late.
>
> — T. S. Eliot in *The Unity of*
> *European Culture*

Quite casually we nodded, shared in talk
Whatever occurred to us, and still the lull
Grew like a bubble till it held all:
Your house, my house; your children on this lawn,
Mine on the other lawn, and in between
As far as we could see there was no line,
Picket, or privet-hedge, or wire wall —
Only this common sundial where you
Sometimes told the time and I too
Divided us. There was no other world.

Then, overnight, all split; each hemisphere
Shut sharply in the better to exclude
All but one view: its own. In every skull
The fissure deepened, yawned interminable,
And every loyal citizen thriftily shored
His neighbor's ruins. Only a little mole
That crept unnoticed under either wall
Too late to matter, treasonous to mind,
As winter deepened the dividing line
Lived in the country of the sundial.

the poet
who talks to himself

The poet who talks to himself
In despair
Or to an audience of
Air,

Married to the poem,
Knows once for all
What nagging lies between
The *will* and the *shall*;

Perceives that beauty is not
Thought, but the object of thought
And dances to its end
Hovering in the wind

Like doves, to settle down
About some casual man
Offering a casual crumb
Or not, as casual can,

Both being portion of
The carelessness of love
Which finds the perfect rhyme
Nowhere and in no time.

the match

'Tis Might, half slumbering on
its own right arm
         — John Keats

Put sinew in it, for it never was
chined prose — that
smells of phosphorescent fat. Your poet
knows sensation and the mind's play
are not the lot: only the only way
to rule all things together, rein and ride
once more over the scared, indignant town
the courser of Medusa's founted blood
and Death's astonishment. With words, then,
common as dirt, but soundly skeletoned
as a good house, resilient as grain
make it if you can; and when your door
thunders and it is Time, invite Time in
and let them try which is the mightier,
he or this Babe who chokes in either hand
a dead serpent that did not understand.

the shapers

Troglodytes, stretched in their cobalt cave,
The clouds loll, lulled by the thrilling music
And lightning logarithms of the wind.

Rapscallions, they loll and do not care
What their wheeling shadows do down here
Engulfing or releasing. A moment ago

I was swallowed by a cloud shadow;
Now sit blinking here in the sun's glare.
The wind's invisible; and yet the wind

Shapes processions of fortuitous cloud
As fortune shapes the mind, or as the tongue
The flux of words that rises from the brain

Shapeless and without form, so I command
And canvas a tall ship to sail the sea.
Its masts break into leaves; its leaves flower

Into a city, tower on white tower,
That would last forever, but the wind
Writhes under my hand; and as stone walls

Alter in spring when the frost melts and thaws,
All comes down. As the wind does to clouds,
The clouds to us, we do

Not as boys drown a miserable kitten
But to reshape anew
All images until they correspond

To the face and image of one man
We know and do not know
Before we pass under the next shadow.

46

do not feed the elephant

O closed in glass, clothed in impenetrable
Crystal, walk among us, gracious
Ice among fever, fresh air among gas,
But whether with peanuts or with *aequitas*

Do not feed the elephant. It is
What it is — a trunk, a leaf, a wall,
A tongueless snake, or two sharp scimitars —
The doctors differ — you alone are free
To watch in silence and be wonderful.

Wound in our webs of wisdom, we can see
Better than you our rich, our eloquent
Subjectivity, but you are sent
That we may freely know our punishment:

Kindly do not feed the elephant.

spring is coming

They say the blood of winter, color of rye,
Shall yet unclot and flow in the streets of spring.
Let the king do as he pleases, live delicately;
Time is *his* king.

But I must get on with my work, consume
This heap of paper on the office table
Steadily, gradually. The room
Is austere and bare, a scholar's room

So let the man knock. I have no lack;
Why should I let him in?
But I can't keep my mind on my work, am not myself
In this uproar.

(All within of course, in the nerves, in the mind.
The king, they say, is half dead, half blind
With the same sound.) Perhaps the visitor
Has friends behind him, and they, friends, and they, friends.

But if I opened the door and the king himself
Flopped forward onto the floor for the spring to breed
Maggots in, weedwheels, wildflowers,
I should go out of my mind,

For terror's phthisic crystal
Cracking all over town with the king's death
Avalanches would roar from a thousand houses,
And I never should get these papers corrected.

swim

The first thing you saw was a man.
He stood on the bank making geometrical figures.
As fast as his finger traced them on the air
The glittering ovals, rhomboids, circles fell
Into the stream and were carried away. The stream
Consisted entirely of them.
And if a few were more opaque than others,
None were so black you could not see the brown
Earth-bed through their swift procession.

You thought yourself quite different at the time,
But looking at involves, and once in
You were carried away. What had seemed mere diagram
Floating about at various distances
Resolved itself while moving side by side
At incredible speed to children, women, men.
You touch, as though at rest, again and again,
And think, "They are a part of me," and dream,
"They are more truly me than I am."

Yet you remember the great artisan
Who never ceased from labor, and know further
You can emerge from the stream at any time
To watch his work. Perhaps it would be better
(Trying is the best philosopher)
To stand on the bank and swim below in the stream
At one and the same time. But having grown
Accustomed to the medium of water
Everything outside appears disorder.

Yet once you did, and therefore must again
Lift a foot, a knee, an eye, a hand

Wholly outside the element and climb
The highest bank to view the waters of
Your last immersion. And as the first
Plunge into water chilled you to the bone,
So on the sand in naked air you'll drown
Until you draw the first deep lungful in.
Air is a thing too clear to be made plain;

Blake's way was to say quite simply:
I bound Time to my left foot like a bright sandal
To walk forward through Eternity.
But could he take it off when he put it on?
Departure is return. The smoky dawn
Will be early still, the maker making,
When you break surface and rear up there,
One foot on the bank, one foot still in,
Knowing your nature is amphibian.

summer unbound

A leaf fell just now,
Bronze as an Indian squaw,
Warm and dead, indubitably so,
Twirling in my office window
It settled on my typewriter, and I

Let it lie. Why should I tap on
Through Indian Summer's satisfaction
With itself, and who am I to disturb
Death's ideal working conditions? Lie
Still, brown leaf. But I,

Closing the door, must carry my conclusions
Past ART and ECONOMICS through the warm
Campus where above me a jet plane
Like a surrealist poet whose metaphor
Exceeds his grasp, outstripping its own rasp,

Inscribes a line tinged by the sinking sun
On the high, blue, Babylonian wall.
I too might crisp and fall
If I could read that bright inscription.
It may be Shelley's friend,

Unbound again, scoops more of the sun's fire
Than that other time
And dives again, inflamed
With pure philanthropy,
Back towards the earth to give it all to men.

handbag

For generations mothers, daughters, grandmothers
Have carried one. Curiously fine
The click it makes, separating time
Past from time present with
Matter-of-factness, tangibility.

When you snapped yours just then, suddenly
I could not think woman grows wholly woman
Until she has one. It has the sound
Of a mind made up before the mind
Knows what it has done. White-armed

Helen must have lifted one just so
And clicked it so when the gray Argive sand
First felt the keel of the black ship from Troy —
And in that moment had already come,
A tall white flame, to kindle Ilium.

PART V · CONSIDERATIONS

the swimmers

Under the sea was our equation:
Language slid from us and our fluid eyes
Welled comfort and despair; under this world
Our crystal and invisible angels
Not without blood altered their idiom.

Dry is the shore, and the sun's paradigm
Declines all shell to shale; inflected fin
Crisps to a curl, drops off, and gill is gone.
Moist, sullen creatures under a damp stone
Slink from the sun's abstraction, but we

Poised on a forked, laborious stratagem,
Plunge inland willy-nilly, far from home,
Engrossing air, swallowing sun, but our
Ensutured caves contain the ocean still:
In every hollow shell we lift to ear

The combers roar, and as we walk the gray
Endlessly hurrying multitude of sand
Equal, particular, and uniform,
Sea saturates our bones' transition;
As we pass through the desert yet we swim.

fall abstract

Autumn was quick this year: the squirrels worked
Harder for acorns; almost everywhere
I saw the scuttle of a furry nation
With button eyes on a foregone conclusion

I cannot see; and all I know is when
My vacuum cleaner with a sudden spurt
Gobbled some tacks the children had left on the floor
I heard machine-gun fire and hit the dirt.

Tonight I saw the moon
Stick in the crotch of the oak outside my house —
But not for long, as I moved it came loose.
Whichever way I turn, wherever I look

Everything seems immortal but the soul
And these oakleaves. I watch them as they fall,
Noting in ugly abstract symbols how
They hightail down at the first touch of frost

(Yet some that rattle like sore throats will cling),
And sometimes when a raker bending down
Kindles them, the coughing and the tears
Sprung from a single, simple seed of flame.

deity

"When I go back . . ."; but the rockfall
Spoiled all that, the air unbreathable
And the tunnel crammed, stuffed with so much
Indubitably rich rubbish, rubbish still
All but impenetrable. But yet note down, Pencil
Of light I write by, neither weak nor strong
But narrowly sufficient, having paused
Long enough by this low wall to see:
That every moment bears the next moment
Out of a womb that snaps like a trap, as hard
As the adamant around us and that God
Is dead in history (perfect) and daily dies
More minutely in all backward eyes;
That only at this end of the passage is
(The wombs being closed that bore us) Deity.

the loss

If I much concern myself with this,
You do too, and all who do not seem
Stone faces dreaming stone's dream
Of nothing, nothing, like the images
On Easter Island. All the animals
Follow us with their eyes as we go by
Wondering what we look for. In the sky
Red fades out to black and the night falls,
Night and the ignorance of eyes; but we
Light matches, matches; on our hands and knees
Ransacking every hummock, every tree's
Droppings for any nickel, dime, or cent
Of the incredible emolument
We never lost until we looked to see.

three ladies

My first is rare and gracious, courtesy
And light and darkness mingle in her face:
She dwells at day's end in a most luminous place:
Food, wine, and lanterns of civility.

My second scorns such gross and bodily
Clinging to houses and rich provender,
Saying it ripens like a yellow pear
Only for others, rots for itself; and she

(My second lady) hunts a dangerous prey
Through harsh, unsettled pastures where burdock
Sticks to her clothes but cannot bar her way
And eats wild grapes, a native of the rock.

My third, in blue, sits on a stone nearby
A little covered basket. The babe in her lap
Lifts in his fists a bunch of grapes which she
Plucks as she will and feeds him grape by grape.

None are for her. Her husband for their fare
Hurls his long staff up into a nut tree
To knock a handful down. The donkey there
Stares at the infant lovingly, sadly.

My first is rich; my second, fleet of foot,
Outstrips the world; my third pities its care.
And all the three are one; the one is three.
There are no other ladies anywhere.

praise for the earthkeepers

Earthkeepers, how agile are your ways,
Your strategies still able to elude
The claws of the mountains that close over us.

All your hot heroes who attempt those tors
And come back shivering, blubbering blood, to say
"That way's impassable! Don't try that way!"

Would never have tried in the first place at all
Did you not know your course
Right from the moment of their setting forth:

And through the longest night, the shortest day
Trim, fill, and set ablaze
Every lamp you have, for thus, they,

Teetering destruction by destruction,
Recall the earthkeepers, and in the daze
And light of light beyond all light, turn,

Cacodemon winds, down, down,
Toward your spark upon the breathable floor
And the doomed valley they have whistled for.

moving

Moving from one poised intelligibility
To another, out of life, out of time,
How anxiously, looking before, behind,
Above, below, we leave the lumpedness,
Substance without form, the Devil's heart
Extended endlessly in pure duree,
The horrible concreteness of living;

The furtive way thoughts creep up from behind
And pounce on us! the beautiful, if true
A panther met, a flicker passing and
Hurting with its blessing. Ugliness,
The shadow cast by all we are and do,
Slinks through the vegetation. Only abstraction,
The swift malevolent whiteness Ahab knew

In bank, bench, legislature, laboratory
Lures us at last, for it is blind as a bat
To flesh and blood, but as old Chekhov said
When someone asked him if he liked the sea:
"Yes. Only it's so empty,"
And stepping poised, stepping delicately,
Added, "The sea is difficult to describe."

snow scene

This is a snow scene on rice paper. (I
Forget the artist's name.) The feathery
Flakes are falling still, and someone
Wearing a snow-peaked coolie-hat shoulders
A snowy burden, and his old horse too

Carries a load that comes to a peak of snow.
Both move toward a village in the pines.
Whether the man who leads the horse is you,
Or whether on immaculate rice paper
In Japan three hundred years ago

You saw it and your brush defined the scene,
You too set black on white, or reading lines
Black on white, shoulder, in an expanse
As innocent as this
A burden that grows always heavier

As you advance
With this piled whiteness, which,
When you look closer
Turns out to be the ground of the whole picture,
Nothing, the clean rice paper showing through.

joy of man's desiring

Needle sliding in the groove,
Resurrect undying love:
Shining metal, turn again —
Past the whisper in the brain
Of its own destruction —
Thought to intuition:

You have reason, Reason none,
For it filters coldly down
Towers black with soot this light
That is neither day nor night
But darkness rational, late star
Of him who shall be Lucifer

Nevermore, and underground,
Mathematically bound,
Fractions all till nova brim
White light over Bethlehem.
Still emerge from the machine
Light that Satan has not seen

On land or sea ; and needle probe
Time's resistance until Love,
Born again in the dull cave
Of our imagination, prove —
Fidelity in more than wiring —
Jesu, joy of man's desiring.

The Amy Lowell Travelling Scholarship Fund made it possible for Mr. Mayo to spend two years recently in England, and it was during this stay that most of these poems were written. He has said of this experience: "During my visit I came to love England and the English people very much, but I'm not at all sure I understand them any better. I hope some of my affection shows in the poems — as well as bewilderment.

"Travel abroad, I have found, tends to intensify one's sens of nationality. It broadens you at least to the extent of helping you realize your own narrowness. At the same time, however, by increasing your detachment, it allows you to see your own nation in a somewhat broader perspective."